fit for
50+

Other books in this series:

Fit for 50+ Shane Gould

fit for 50+

GREG CHAPPELL

ibis publishing
AUSTRALIA

Always consult your doctor before beginning an exercise program.

Published by Ibis Publishing Australia
Level One, 257 Coventry Street
South Melbourne, Victoria 3205 Australia

www.ibispublishing.com.au
info@ibispublishing.com.au

National Library of Australia
Cataloguing-in-Publication

Chappell, Greg, 1948- .
Fit for 50+ : exercises for men who want to live well for longer.

ISBN 1 920923 18 7.

1. Exercise for middle aged persons. 2. Physical fitness for middle
aged persons. 3. Middle aged men - Health and hygiene. I. Title. II.
title : Fit for fifty plus. III. Title : Fit for 50 plus. IV. title : Fit for
fifty +.

613.70449

Illustrations by Karen Carter
Printed in Australia by Griffin Press

Contents

If you were to survey every man aged between forty and seventy in Australia, you would find that a majority of them, perhaps nearly all of them, would like to be healthier and fitter than they are. The trouble is they don't know where to start.

Inactivity: a mindset

There is no doubt the mental side of the equation is as important as the physical. Once you start even thinking that you can't do something, it won't be long before you can't *physically* do it.

The problem is surrendering to the physical decline that people traditionally associate with aging. There is a general acceptance that beyond the age of fifty your body starts to run down like an old car. People take it for granted that at that age they will become less and less active, that they'll have to go to the doctor more often and that they'll suffer from all kinds of pains and minor disabilities they didn't have before.

Attitude is everything. If you have the idea that when you reach fifty you enter a twilight zone where the sun is setting, you're half-finished already. But if you approach this age with the idea that it's a time of opportunity, you are sure to enjoy it and will probably find it particularly productive.

Time for a change of approach

In my own case, I consciously approached this period as a time when, free from previous encumbrances, I would be able to enter new fields, attempt new ventures and generally make some changes in my life. I saw it as a time of challenge. This is how it has turned out. In my mid- to late-forties, I sold out of several businesses that had been a big part of my life for many years. I moved house. I entered into a couple of ventures that were entirely new to me. And I changed my eating habits and with them, my lifestyle.

There was a temptation to stay in the comfort zone and just coast along, without trying anything new. I'm pleased now I resisted it. I have a special admiration for those people we meet or hear about who have struck out in new directions. Winston Churchill was one. He was hardly a picture of

Energy is one commodity we do not have to lose as we move through life.

robust health, but he did have the right attitude. In the 1920s, when he was over fifty years old, he took up bricklaying, having signed on as an adult apprentice of the bricklayers' union. He built a summer house and high garden walls, which you can still see if you visit his country home, Chartwell.

Improved energy levels

Whether or not Churchill had much physical energy, he certainly had plenty of mental energy. In fact, the two usually go hand in hand. Energy is one commodity we do not have to lose as we move through life. My own energy levels were quite low in my twenties, and they started to rise only after I changed my eating habits. Today, having passed fifty, I certainly have more energy than I had twenty-five years ago; not the kind of energy you need for a ten kilometre run, of course, but the energy you need to do the ordinary, day-to-day activities that fill our lives. This is the kind of energy that we all need to have.

The importance of mental image

There comes a time in life when you feel like staying in the chair and when you are entitled to stay in that chair. But you cannot, must not, stay in the chair indefinitely. It is vital that you maintain a mental image of yourself as an active person. In a sense, maintaining this image of yourself is just as important as actually being active. If you think of yourself as an active person you will stay active. Conversely, if you start thinking of yourself as a couch potato, a couch potato is certainly what you will become. If you're convinced you've reached an age at which aches and stiffness are inevitable, you can be sure your body will ache and your joints feel stiff.

If you think of yourself as an active person you will stay active.

The importance of self-image for the older man cannot be overstressed. Everyone reading this will be able to think of someone who is not so old in years but decidedly old in mind and in manner. You can see them any day of the week—younger men who stand, move about and generally conduct themselves like older men. Even their faces wear aged, worn-out expressions.

On the other hand, we can all think of men of the opposite type: men brimming with vitality who might be in their seventies but move and speak as decisively as someone twenty years younger. If you could look into their heads I am sure you would find that in every case these men genuinely think of themselves as robust and energetic. That's the key to their energy levels.

Is it a state of mind?

Do you lose the will, the spirit, to be active before you lose the physical ability to be active? My personal view is that middle-age usually begins as a state of mind. That said, it is obvious that your state of mind is affected by your physical condition. It would be silly to try to maintain a youthful state of mind indefinitely in the hope of remaining youthfully fit and vigorous. Your state of mind must change. Mine has certainly changed. I have tried hard over the years to remain physically capable, yet I often find myself, when offered the chance of joining in some physical activity that I used to enjoy, deciding that it's not for me. This is only natural.

Being prepared

Consider the case of the fellow who decides to stay in his chair instead of kicking the football. If he's over fifty, he is perfectly entitled to stay in the chair if this happens to be his preference on that particular day. The important thing is that when the day comes that he wants to kick the football, he ought to be physically capable of doing it. I believe this ought to be an objective of every older man. Throughout our fifties, sixties and beyond we ought to be able to exert ourselves physically when we want to—to climb onto the roof to clear the gutters or maybe play a game of beach cricket—without the fear of hurting ourselves and feeling stiff, sore and sorry for days afterwards.

Throughout our fifties, sixties and beyond we ought to be able to exert ourselves physically when we want to.

Ready for anything

I experienced a personal example of this not that long ago. Several members of my younger son's A-grade baseball team went off to play in the national championships, which left the team a couple of players short for a forthcoming game. When it seemed the team would have to forfeit the match, I suggested to one of the other fathers, who like me, had played baseball in his youth, that we should fill the gap. The problem was we had no pitcher, so I volunteered to do the job. We played, and I pitched nine innings in the game. I took a hiding, but it was great fun. Indeed, I had forgotten just how much fun you can have doing something as simple as running about and throwing and hitting a ball.

I had done a lot of stretching and it clearly had paid off.

I was forty-eight years old at the time. For a few weeks

before the game I prepared myself for the pitching with some light throwing practice. But I had not pitched as such in thirty years, and nine innings is a lot of pitching for anyone of any age. For the last two or three innings I struggled, but I made it through, and afterwards I went for a run and did some stretching exercises.

I'd kept active during this time with both a daily exercise program and a walking program.

The big test was going to be how I pulled up over the next few days. Well, I woke next morning and felt fine. This was encouraging, but it's usually on the second day that aches and stiffness are the worst. The second day came and I still felt fine. My throwing arm and shoulder were not sore at all; nor were my back and legs. Strangely, I ached in only one place, my left buttock, and this was obviously because I had thrown all my weight over my left leg each time I pitched.

I was pleasantly surprised at how well I had weathered it all. I felt pleased with myself. I had done hardly any running in the previous ten years, but I'd kept active during this time with both a daily exercise program and a walking program, which I had stuck to faithfully. In particular, I had done a lot of stretching. All this, it now seemed, had paid off. Playing baseball that day wasn't something I had planned to do. It isn't something I may necessarily want to do again. The point is, though, that when the need arose, when I wanted to do it, I was able to do it.

Did you ever see your father run?

A friend about my own age once made an interesting observation to me. He said he didn't ever see his father run, and he speculated that this was because men of his father's generation considered it somehow undignified to break out of a walk once they passed, say, fifty. As a boy I used to watch my father play grade cricket in Adelaide when he must have been about forty years old. After that, though, I cannot remember him ever going faster than a walk.

Consciously or subconsciously, my father's generation thought they were past it.

There may be some truth in my friend's observation. I think

men of previous generations did regard running as some-how beneath them. I strongly suspect this was because of the mindset I referred to earlier; that is, the acceptance of physical decline. Consciously or subconsciously, they thought they were past it. Running was something boys and young men did.

Happily, this idea changed long ago. For twenty-five years now joggers of every age have been a familiar sight. (In fact, for reasons I will discuss later they would really be better off walking than jogging.) In other ways, though, that mindset has not changed.

The pay-off

By the time we hit fifty most of us have already achieved social and financial security or are well on the way to doing so, and are starting to enjoy the freedom that comes when children grow up and begin fending for themselves. We are free of the need to prove ourselves, which makes the twenties and thirties such a stressful time of life. We are free of

The tragedy is that many of us are no longer fit enough to enjoy our middle age.

the need to push and shove as we climb our career ladder. We are free, or soon will be, of the financial burden and other obligations of having children at school. We are free to start doing the things we always wanted to do but for which we somehow never had enough time or money.

In short, this should be the time when you start receiving the pay-off from all that hard slog. In some ways, life as we live it seems back to front. When we're young and have the time and energy to do things, we don't have the money. After that, while we're raising a family and buying a house, we have neither the time nor the money. Then, at last we have the time and the money to play golf regularly again, or to join a bushwalking club as we always planned to do, or go on that often-talked-about trip to Europe, or finally teach ourselves the guitar, or to start spending weekends away. The tragedy is that many of us are no longer fit enough, active enough, healthy enough or energetic enough to do any of these things.

The pleasures foregone

I have no grandchildren as yet, but I look forward very much to having them and doing things with them. I suspect there are many men of about my age with sons and daughters that are grown up or almost grown up, who now regret not spending more time with them while they were children. The reason, in my own case, was that as an

At last we have the time and the money to do the things we've always wanted to.

international sportsman I was away for many months each year. Career commitments no doubt affect many other men in the same way. Now one has the opportunity to make amends for previous omissions by spending a lot of time with one's grandchildren, but, again, to do this you have to be mobile enough to keep up with them, physically and mentally.

The fitness goal

The great thing about fitness in middle age is that it's not so hard to achieve. What you have to do is change your eating habits, walk regularly and exercise regularly. You don't have to enrol at a gym or invest in expensive exercising equipment. We've all seen those exercise

It's not hard to prolong an active middle age

machines advertised on television. Millions of dollars have been spent on these contraptions, most of which are rusting in the garage. As I'll explain later you can build a home gym that will provide everything you need at virtually no cost.

How to prolong your active middle age?

- Eat nutritious food.
- Walk regularly
- Exercise regularly

This has all been said before, but it's important enough to be worth repeating.

The problem of modern living

The need to make a special effort to keep fit is one of the penalties of modern living. There was a time when people got all the exercise they needed just going about the business of their normal daily lives. If you thought that the men who were the cricket greats of the 1920s spent a lot of time training you'd be wrong. Apart from practice in the nets, most cricketers did no training at all. They did not run laps of the oval or work out in whatever kind of gyms were

Today very few middle-aged men are naturally fit. Fitness can only be attained by exercising.

available then. They didn't have exercise programs either.

These men lived far more active lives than men of today. They would have climbed stairs instead of using lifts and escalators, cut lawns with push-mowers, walked to the local shop instead of driving, walked to the post box instead of sending an email, and quite possibly walked to and from work. They did not need to run around the oval. They were naturally fit.

Exercise programs

Today very few middle-aged men are naturally fit. Fitness is a condition we can attain only by exercising. You could fill a library with the books and articles that have been written over the past thirty years on this subject. The number of exercise programs they contain must run into thousands. But there are very few programs suited to men over fifty.

Wellbeing

We exercise for the benefit of our bodies, of course, but we should not overlook the feel-good factor. Most men who exercise regularly, myself included, experience it to some degree — an ongoing feeling of personal satisfaction and well-being. It's not an easy feeling to define, but when it's present it's unmistakable. You feel good about yourself, you feel more alive, you feel invigorated. Nobody knows for sure if it has a chemical or psychological origin, aand it doesn't really matter. The important thing is that exercising not only does you good but also makes you feel good.

When you don't exercise, you feel bad about yourself.

There is a converse side to all this. When you don't exercise, you feel bad about yourself. You keep thinking to yourself: 'You lazy bastard, why don't you get up and go for a walk?'

So you live with a vague feeling of guilt, which over a period must have a negative effect on your attitude to yourself and to your outlook on life in general.

Reverse tiredness

Exercise can have a strangely invigorating effect in the short term, too. If you come home feeling worn out and throw yourself into a chair, you will continue to feel worn out. But if, instead, you jump up and do ten minutes' vigorous walking or exercising—admittedly the last thing you would ordinarily feel like doing in this situation—the feeling of exhaustion disappears. I know the idea of exercising to overcome exhaustion sounds contradictory, but I've tried it many times and it always works. There is one precondition, of course: you must be reasonably fit to start with.

Health benefits

The good news is that several studies have shown that it's never too late to get fit. An exercise regime for over fifties has a myriad of health benefits, including:

- reducing the risk of serious diseases such as heart disease, diabetes and colon cancer

- reduced cholesterol and high blood pressure

- increasing your sense of wellbeing and reducing depression and anxiety

- helping you maintain a healthy weight

- building and maintaining healthy bones, muscles and joints

- helping you manage some existing health conditions and preventing their reoccurrence

- improving your quality of life and reducing the risk of dying prematurely

The amount and size of muscles decrease with age. We lose around three kilograms of lean muscle every decade from middle age. But this loss may be related to a sedentary lifestyle, rather than age. Older people can increase their muscle mass quickly by exercising regularly.

It's never too late to get fit! Regular exercise has a myriad of health benefits.

A fit seventy-year-old who has stayed active is probably as strong and fit as a sedentary thirty-year-old. Active people decline physiologically by about half a per cent a year, whereas inactive people decline by about two per cent.

Regular exercise not only increases muscle mass, but also burns kilojoules and speeds your metabolism. Being overweight can lead to a range of diseases including cardio-vascular disease and diabetes.

Bone density also begins to decline after forty, and this loss accelerates at around fifty. As a result, older people are more susceptible to breaking bones. Weight-bearing exercise helps to keep bones healthy and strong.

Regular exercise increases muscle mass, burns kilojoules and speeds your metabolism.

Your joints need regular move-ment to remain supple and healthy. Regular flexibility exer-cises strengthen soft tissue, such as tendons and ligaments, and thus reduce the risk of injuries.

Regardless of your age, you can improve your heart and lung fit-ness by regular, moderate intensity exercise. It may take longer to achieve results than for a young person, but the physical benefits are similar.

It's a widely held belief that only vigorous and sustained exercise can bring health benefits. This attitude prevents a lot of people from ever starting to exercise. Fortunately it's not true. You can get a significant boost to your health from regular moderate physical activity.

Osteoporosis

Osteoporosis is a disease where the bones become brittle and prone to fractures. The loss of bone density is gradual. Often there are no warning signs until the disease is advanced. Once osteoporosis sets in even minor falls can cause serious fractures.

Osteoporosis is a very real risk for all Australians. Fractures from osteoporosis are a major cause of illness, long term disability and death in older Australians.

Osteoporosis is a very real risk for all over fifties.

Exercise is an important factor in bone strength. Bones need the mechanical stress of physical activity to keep strong. Regular exercise keeps bones strong and maintains bone density. Your muscles also stay strong, your joints are flexible and your balance is good, further reducing the chance of falls and injury.

Osteoporosis experts recommend a combination of high impact, strengthening, weight-bearing, and balance and coordination exercises to help prevent the development of osteoporosis. The exercise must be regular and

The exercise must be regular and continuous for the beneficial effects on bone density to last.

continuous as the beneficial effects on bone density only last as long as the exercise continues.

Balance

As we get older, a major benefit of exercise is preventing falls. By exercising our balance and coordination we can improve our stability and avoid falls, which are responsible for many hip fractures and other injuries.

To maintain your balance, it has to be tested. You need to get off the vertical in a safe way, and keep giving your brain the experience of being out of balance so it can practice adapting to that.

Exercising our balance is an important part of exercise.

Anything that is unstable, such as sitting on a ball, challenges your balance. Using an inflatable fit (or Swiss) ball is an excellent way to improve your balance and build your stability. You can use one as part of your exercise regime or just sit on it when you are working at your desk, eating dinner or watching TV.

Pelvic floor muscles

One of the unfortunate side-effects of getting older is weakening muscles and one set of muscles that we don't want weakening are the pelvic floor muscles. This can lead to urinary incontinence, as the pelvic floor muscles play an important role in bladder control.

Weak pelvic floor muscles can contribute to incontinence in men just as it does in women.

However regular pelvic floor muscle exercises can ensure you remain free of this embarrassing condition. They are recommended for both older men and women. If you're overweight, you are particularly prone to urinary incontinence because every kilo adds more pressure to your bladder.

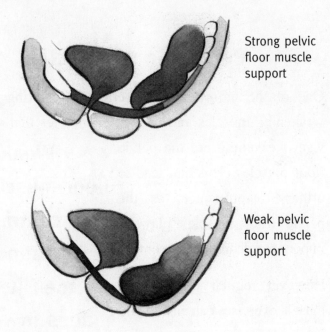

Strong pelvic
floor muscle
support

Weak pelvic
floor muscle
support

To locate your pelvic floor muscles

Lie on your back with your knees bent. To locate the pelvic
floor muscles firstly tighten the ring of muscles around the
back passage as if you are trying to control wind or diarrhoea.

Try not to squeeze your buttocks. Relax and feel the difference when you relax the muscle.

Now tighten the whole pelvic floor — around your anus and bladder—as though you are trying to stop passing urine. Hold as long as you can then relax. Now repeat and count how long you can hold the contraction. If your muscle is weak it may only be two seconds, or you may be able to hold for ten seconds if you have good control. The contraction should feel like an upward inward movement, but if the muscle is very weak it will be just a small squeeze. You will also feel tension in your lower abdomen as this deep stomach muscle contracts simultaneously with your pelvic floor muscles. A strong muscle will produce a squeezing and drawing up feeling.

A strong muscle contraction should feel like an upward inward movement.

For more information on urinary incontinence and pelvic floor muscle exercises see the Australian Continence Website at www.continence.health.gov.au.

Diabetes

Diabetes is a chronic condition where there is too much glucose (sugar) in the blood. Type II diabetes (sometimes called adult-onset diabetes) is the most prevalent form of diabetes and it affects close to one million Australians over the age of twenty-five. It's more common in people over forty-five and around 150 people are being diagnosed daily.

Type II diabetes is more common in people over forty-five.

With Type II diabetes, the body still produces insulin, but there may be less of it or it may not work properly. This results in disturbances to the carbohydrate, fat and protein metabolism which can damage the body's systems, especially the blood vessels and nerves. Complications can include nerve damage, loss of vision and heart disease. It is also associated with a cluster of problems including high blood pressure, high cholesterol and obesity. Diabetes is the seventh biggest killer in Australian and its occurrence is rising rapidly.

Type II diabetes is a 'modern lifestyle disease', which means it's brought on by inactivity, poor nutrition and obesity. Currently there's no cure. However it may be preventable by leading a healthy lifestyle, which means enjoying a nutritious diet and plenty of physical activity. Another very good reason to get and stay fit!

Diabetes is the seventh biggest killer and its occurrence is rising rapidly.

The latest research says that progressive strength training is highly beneficial for people with Type II diabetes. Regular strength training can lower blood glucose levels, as well as increase muscle strength and size, decrease body fat and improve self-esteem.

This is great news for anyone who has Type II diabetes or is in a high risk group because:

- Lowering blood glucose levels reduces the risk of future complications.

- Lowering blood glucose levels can delay or prevent the onset of Type II diabetes in people who are at high risk.

- Increasing muscle size helps the body to be more metabolically active (burning extra energy), allowing people to be more energetic and helping them to lose fat.

For more information on diabetes, check out the Diabetes Australia website at www.diabetesaustralia.com.au.

The need to be active

I have changed from being someone who exercised in fits and starts as my enthusiasm for it waxed and waned to someone who sticks to a program faithfully, month after month. Frankly, I would not dare do otherwise. I recognise that now in my fifties I have reached a stage in life where I need to keep active if I want to remain active. If I were to get lazy and go for a month or two without exercising, I know I'd be on a downhill slide. The slide might start slowly, but with each month it would get steeper and steeper and before long I'd be joining the ranks of clapped-out middle-aged men. True, I could always stop the slide

> **I have reached a stage in life where I need to keep active if I want to remain active.**

and start exercising again, but I would have lost valuable ground, and to recover that lost ground would not be easy.

Quality life

The walking routine and the exercises are therefore not intended as a quick fix for the unfit. They are a program for the long haul. You really need to follow them or some similar program for the rest of your life. If you do, the quality of your life will be immeasurably better and you will be happy living longer.

Regardless of your age, you can improve heart and lung fitness with regular moderate exercise.

There is little to be said for living twenty years longer if for most of this time you are unwell and find it hard to get around. All you will have managed to do is extend your old age. But if you extend your life by twenty years by extending your *middle age* by twenty years, then it will be a longer life worth living.

Good nutrition

When we enter middle age we are at one of life's most important crossroads. We can allow our body to continue its middle-age decline, growing fatter and slower, suffering more illnesses, and becoming less active; or we can arrest the process by bold intervention. By changing certain areas of our lifestyle, we can make ourselves fitter and healthier, and by doing this we can ensure not only that we stay active throughout our middle age but that we prolong this active middle age far beyond the normal span.

What you put in your mouth contributes to how rapidly you age, how energetic you feel, how sick you are, how fat you grow and how soon you die. By adopting new eating habits and by committing yourself to regular exercise you can transform yourself physically and, perhaps, change your mental outlook too.

Eating nutritious food is really one of the keys to good health. It means not only eating more good food (vegetables, fruit and complex carbohydrates such as breads and

What you eat can contribute to how rapidly you age.

pasta) but also less bad food. Generally, you need to cut your consumption of animal protein to a minimum. In fact, the closer you come to a vegetarian style of eating, the better your chance of achieving optimum health.

Saturated animal fats

It ought to be stressed that this does not mean everyone should become a vegetarian. Not everyone is suited to the vegetarian style of eating, physically or emotionally. But there is no doubt that everyone could benefit by consuming less protein, especially if the protein has an animal source and therefore contains a lot of saturated fat and cholesterol.

The basics seem simple: we should eat less protein and we should eat more fruit, vegetables and complex carbo-hydrates, the last of which are rich in fibre.

Lower cholesterol

According to one calculation, the normal Western diet con-tains three times more protein than is needed. We could reduce our protein intake by two-thirds and still have enough! Even someone on a pure vegetarian diet is liable to consume too much protein. Some vegetables are rich in protein, especially the pulses—beans, peas, lentils, chickpeas and the tofu products used frequently by vegetarians. The important

We could reduce our protein intake by two-thirds and still have enough!

thing is that plant protein contains none of the saturated fats and cholesterol that are found in animal protein.

Diet benefits

It is a common experience for middle-aged people who have cut down on meat and dairy products to find they no longer suffer from the indigestion that had been afflicting them for years. There is a simple explanation for this.

Animal products tend to acidify the body's system.

Animal products tend to acidify the system. By reducing the intake of animal products, you reduce the acidity, which in turn results in a disappearance of indigestion. The fact is that all foods except raw fruits and vegetables are acid-forming but animal protein is the most acid-forming.

Guidelines

It is hard to be too specific about what an ideal diet should consist of, given that each of us is different from everyone else, but broad guidelines are certainly available. A recommended breakdown by quantity (weight, not volume) of the kinds of food we should eat each day to achieve optimum health are: fresh fruit and vegetables 75 per cent; starchy foods (bread, potatoes, pumpkin, rice) 10 per cent; protein-rich foods (meat, cheese, eggs, nuts, legumes) 7.5 per cent; sugar-rich foods (sugar, honey, dried fruits) 5 per cent; fat-rich foods (oil, margarine, butter, cream) 2.5 per cent.

Fresh fruit and vegetables should comprise three-quarters of your diet

Fresh fruit and vegetables should comprise about three-quarters of your diet if you wish to eat as healthily as possible. This leads to a further question: what fruit and vegetables, specifically, should you eat and in which proportion? The short answer is that it does not really matter. Provided you eat a reasonable range of them you need not worry too much. Variety is the key. For instance, if apples and bananas are the only fruit you eat, then your range of fruit is deficient.

Nutrients in plant foods

Here are a few other points to keep in mind. If you are

Raw fruits and vegetables provide the body with essential enzymes.

switching to a pure or mainly vegetarian style of eating, you will need to include iron-rich plant foods in your diet. This isn't difficult.

Green leafy vegetables are a good source of iron, and of

these raw spinach is about the best. Broccoli and cabbage are excellent, and cucumber, cauliflower, lettuce and beet tops are good, too.

Fruit is another good source of iron. Here, in order, are some of the highest: strawberries, apricots, lemons, blueberries and pineapple. Also, try to include a number of orange-coloured fruits and vegetables (citrus fruits, carrots, sweet potatoes, mangoes) in your diet, because these contain betacarotene, which is converted to vitamin A in the body. As for vitamin C—well, most fruits and vegetables, especially in their raw form, contain this important vitamin in some degree. Citrus fruits and juices, blackcurrants, broccoli and brussels sprouts are particularly good sources.

Food that is raw has much greater nutritional value.

There are other reasons for eating raw fruit and vegetables. Raw fruit and vegetables also provide the body with essential enzymes which the body otherwise has to manufacture itself at considerable cost.

Changing diet

I realise most people would find it hard to switch suddenly to a diet consisting mainly of raw fruit and vegetables, but it is nevertheless the goal to aim for.

One of the rewards of becoming pro-active in attaining good health and an improved diet is the knowledge you are reducing the chance of contracting life-shortening illnesses like heart disease or cancer. Striving for good health does not guarantee you will avoid cancer or

Be proactive and strive for good health and fitness.

some other illness, but at least you will no longer feel like a sitting duck waiting for the illness to strike.

Losing weight

If you eat less or if you eat the same but eat better, you will certainly lose weight. You often hear overweight men insisting they do not eat much, and the usual reason for this is that they are really talking about the food they eat at meal-times. They ignore the food they eat between meals as if it did not count. If you were to look into the matter you would often find that these men eat three or four snacks a day and that the snacks they eat are fattening: ice-cream, bars of chocolate, bags of hot chips. Do not fool yourself into believing that because of your physical

Attaining good health reduces the chance of contracting a life-shortening illness.

make-up you cannot lose weight, no matter how hard you try.

If you follow the basic rules of good nutrition and if you keep active, your weight will drop whether you want it to or not.

Walking:
the preferable alternative

Mike Agostini, the former sprint champion and fitness expert, wrote a book called *How to Avoid Killing Yourself: The dangers of being a fitness fanatic*. It contains a warning for people who are inactive and then, on reaching middle age suddenly decide to try to get fit. He warns that some will have developed coronary disease and not be aware of it, so they risk killing themselves in the attempt to become healthier. They also risk injuring or even maiming themselves.

A man of fifty-eight can be fitter than one aged twenty-eight.

Agostini cites research showing that middle-aged people should not exercise hard on any two consecutive days, the reason being that the middle-aged body takes up to thirty-six hours to fully recover from this kind of exercise.

This is consistent with my own experience. When I cast my mind back to people I knew of roughly my own age who have died over the past fifteen years or so, I am surprised at how many of them died running. In fact, *most* of those who died suddenly in this age bracket died running. The statistics support this impression. Some time ago an American survey was reported in the press which showed that a surprisingly high proportion of men who died suddenly between the ages of forty and sixty died while running or having sex. I mentioned this to a middle-aged friend, a former sportsman. 'I'd better give up running!' he said.

Extend your middle age by twenty years, then it will be a longer life worth living.

Mike Agostini's overall message is nevertheless positive.

He writes: 'Some studies have suggested that a man of fifty-eight can indeed be fitter and thus, in effect, 'younger' than one aged twenty-eight if the older person maintains a sound fitness regime while the other does little or nothing.'

I agree entirely. I am fitter now in an overall sense than I was when I competed internationally. Many other active, middle-aged men could say something similar. A recent health report also confirmed that being fit even while being overweight reduces the chances of suffering illnesses such as heart disease and cancer.

Being fit reduces the chances of suffering illnesses like heart disease.

Running is for the birds

I would not try too hard to persuade a man who has been running for years to stop it. But I would certainly try to persuade someone who has been inactive for years not to take it up. This isn't just because of the obvious risk of having a heart attack or damaging joints. There are other, little-recognised health risks inherent in vigorous exertion in middle age. One is potential damage from chemical particles in the body called free radicals. Free radicals can cause disease and otherwise harm the body in countless ways, and strenuous exercise is known to accelerate

There is plenty of evidence that you only need to walk for 20 minutes for it to be of benefit.

their intake and their production by the body. This is a particularly important consideration in middle age, when the body's natural defence against free radicals has begun to weaken.

Walking

A much preferable alternative is brisk walking. By walking, you enjoy most of the health benefits of running without incurring the health risks of running. There is evidence to show that even in middle age you need to walk for at least twenty minutes to make the exercise really worthwhile, although my own view is that a ten-minute or even five-minute walk is much better than nothing.

Dr Ken Cooper, the American doctor and author who helped launch the fitness craze in the late 1960s, points out in his book, *The Antioxidant Revolution*, that a really fast walker—that is, one who can go as fast as a jogger—actually burns off more calories per kilometre than a jogger.

I do no running at all, but I do a lot of walking. I normally play golf twice a week, which ensures I get a good walk on at least two days in seven, and on top of this I try to walk for twenty minutes or more on at least two other days.

Ideally, you ought to walk briskly to lift your pulse rate and exercise your heart. For the same reason, try to include a hill or two in your route—provided, of course, you are up to it. You should not exert yourself to a point where you cannot talk while you walk. Don't puff yourself out.

As we all know, walking burns up energy and so burns up fat — provided you do it regularly. A brisk walk raises our metabolic rate by more than most of us realise. Oxygen intake is probably the best measure of this. If you are sitting in a chair, your body will probably be using about a third of a litre of oxygen per minute. If you get out of the chair and stride down the street, the rate of usage is likely to climb to one and a third litres of oxygen per minute; that is, three to four times as much.

Ideally, you ought to walk briskly to lift your pulse rate and exercise your heart.

For many years scientists have believed that the body's metabolic rate remained higher than normal long after the exercise was finished, a phenomenon which was sometimes referred to as 'after glow'. Thus, a twenty-minute walk a day ensured that your body burned up fat for, say, twenty-four hours. Unfortunately, research at Flinders University in South Australia by the sports scientist Dr Christopher Gore has all but debunked this theory. Dr Gore found that the 'after glow' effect of walking or even running was minimal.

Regular walking combined with a healthy diet helps you control your weight.

This may be disappointing for walkers, yet, as Dr Gore himself says, it does not alter the fact that, apart from other benefits such as the reduced risk of cardiovascular disease, regular walking combined with a healthy food intake helps you control body weight.

Burn off the kilograms

The key word here is 'regular'. Dr Gore's research shows that it takes thirty half-hour walks to burn off one kilogram of body fat. In other words, if you were to walk for thirty minutes a day on five days a week it would take you six weeks to burn off a kilogram of fat. This may seem slow progress, but it also means that if you did it for a year you would burn off nearly nine kilograms, or about a stone and a half. Of course, if you also take action on the nutrition front by reducing your intake of fat and protein, your weight may drop much faster.

Just by walking 30 minutes a day, five days a week, can burn off one kilogram of fat in six weeks.

Different approaches

Walking is an idiosyncratic activity. Some men like to follow exactly the same route around surrounding streets and parks, year in year out. Others like to vary the route each time they set off. Some prefer to walk early in the morning before showering and dressing for work. Others prefer the cool of the evening and, perhaps, the cover of darkness.

Plan to walk rather than drive—it's an easy way to get aerobic exercise.

A journalist friend of mine who tried and failed for years to settle into a regular walking routine finally had success when he bought a Walkman-style radio and began listening to classical music as he walked around. From then on, he says, his daily walk became not a task but a pleasure.

Then there are those who exercise in probably the most

efficient way of all—they walk to and from work. Presumably they are people with access to showering and changing facilities at the office. I once read of a man who walked ten kilometres from his home to his office in a big city every morning and then walked home at night yet he got there quicker than he could have by a peak-hour bus.

If you think of yourself as an active person you will stay active.

Some men prefer using machines such as exercise bikes and treadmills to walking. This is fine, provided they keep at it. My general reservation about exercise machines (apart from the fact that they can cost a lot of money) is that the people who use them often do not persist with them. When the novelty wears off, the machine disappears into the garage, never to be seen again.

The rebounder

There is one machine I do recommend. It is a small, circular trampoline known variously as a rebounder, rebound jogger or simply mini-trampoline. You need to buy one that is reasonably strong (the springs tend to give out in the cheaper models). Jogging on a rebounder is an excellent alternative to walking when walking is difficult, perhaps because the weather is too hot, too cold or too wet. It's a

Drag yourself out of the chair and do some exercise while watching television.

good idea to buy one and put it on the floor next to the chair where you normally sit to watch television. If there's a half-hour show that you watch each night—the news, for instance—make a point of dragging your rump out of the chair and jogging on the rebounder while you watch the television. You need not do anything strenuous. If it suits you, just imitate the shuffle that long-distance runners use.

Jogging on the rebounder is an excellent exercise and it does not jar the knees and ankles. There can be no excuse

What is your body age? The good news is that it's never too late to get fit.

for not doing it, either, for everyone can spare at least a half-hour per day to watch television. There may well be an extra health benefit, too. Each time your body rises off the rebounder there is a momentary period of weightlessness, which it is said aids the flow in your lymphatic system.

I began using a rebounder while I was in my thirties—years before I began walking regularly. When I turned forty, I went to a clinic to get an executive fitness test done. After the test I sat opposite the specialist in charge of the clinic while he filled out a form with my results. The last part of the form to be filled in was headed 'Body Age', and naturally I was very interested to see what he would write. In fact, he wrote 'forty'. I was disappointed. As a former international sportsman who had been playing golf regularly and using the rebounder, I was immodest enough to believe that my body was young for its years. I thought he might have written 'thirty-two' or, at worst, 'thirty-five'.

He noticed my disappointment and asked what the matter was. I told him I had hoped for a better result. 'I wouldn't worry if I were you,' he said. 'I test a lot of forty-year-olds here, and for most of them I have to write fifty-four or sixty-two. You're miles ahead of the game. You must do a lot of running, do you?' I told him that, no, I didn't run, but I did use a rebounder. 'Well, whatever you're doing,' he said, 'keep doing it, because it works.'

I did keep doing it. I am still using a rebounder today.

Doing exercises

For some reason, most people have an aversion to doing exercises. They may be willing to change their eating habits and walk four times a week, but suggest to them that they spend even five minutes a day doing exercises and at once they lose interest. The reason, probably, is that most people do not really believe that exercises do them any good. They view them as a kind of

An exercise regime for over fifties has a myriad of health benefits.

ritual people do out of a sense of duty but which actually produce little, if any, practical benefit. They're wrong. Exercises do make a difference. They produce a real, practical benefit which can significantly affect your wellbeing. Doing exercises has certainly made a big difference to me. I know it, because I have felt it.

Stretching

The exercises that follow are essentially stretching exercises. What they are intended to do is to keep all your moving parts in good working order. They are invaluable in preserving the body's flexibility, which is one of the first things that men start to lose.

If you own a cat, you will already know a good deal about stretching. Cats stretch themselves many times each day, and like everything else animals do by instinct there's a good reason for it. Stretching elongates the muscle fibres, which is one reason

As we grow older, we need to maintain our flexibility.

it is so effective in maintaining flexibility. Stretching also tends to calm the mind. Stretching relaxes muscles and so has a relaxing overall effect on the body. This in turn produces a general feeling of wellbeing. Five minutes of stretching in the middle of a busy day can do wonders for your disposition.

Five minutes that can change your world

Every day I try to do some stretching, preferably at a time when I need to get away from it all, even for a few minutes. Stretching releases the tension held in the muscles, and makes exercising easier. It helps warm up the muscles and enables you to perform better with better muscle function.

Research shows that stretching helps prevent injuries.

When I was running a company in Sydney I used to spend five minutes stretching during office hours each day. I soon worked out that the only way to make sure I did it every day was to allocate the time for it in my diary. In other words, I made an appointment for myself to do it. At the chosen moment, usually early in the afternoon, I would close the door, lie on the floor and go through a series of stretching exercises.

Consistency, not hard work, gets lasting results.

Real progress is made by stretching every day, but even if you manage only two times a week, you will reap the rewards.

By exercising with regular stretches the agony of tight and sore muscles will eventually disappear—often for good—and it will improve your posture too.

Total relaxation

After stretching I often like to lie still, breathing deeply and allowing myself to relax and drift off into that twilight zone between being awake and asleep. I find this brief period of total relaxation has an energising effect on me. At the end of it I feel charged up and ready to go.

Exercise:
a three part program

There are three parts to a healthy program.

One consists of walking, which I do three or four times a week.

The second consists of muscle toning, which I try to do every day.

The third consists of exercise routines, mainly stretches, which I do first thing in the morning and last thing at night.

Exercise twice a day

The exercises that follow are in two groups. Those in the first group are meant to be done in the morning as you are getting out of bed. The second can be done at the end of the day. There is a reason, apart from convenience, for doing exercises in bed in the morning. Basically, the exercises are intended to get your body moving after a night in bed and this time is when your body is at its most relaxed. The hip exercises loosen up the lower back, a vulnerable area for most men, especially if they spend most of their working day sitting. The evening exercises tend to relax the body, so they will help you get a good night's rest.

The important thing is that all the following exercises must be done slowly and thoroughly. Try to keep this in mind at all times.

Morning Program

Start the day with some stretches.

Important things to remember

Start by doing each exercise in the Morning and Afternoon/Evening Program once or twice and increase the number as your flexibility improves. None of the exercises should cause pain and you should not persist with any that do. You should be aware of the sensation of stretch but not pain.

Your body needs oxygen to function at its best. Inhale through your nose, exhale through your mouth. Remember to exhale on exertion—don't 'hold' your breath.

Exercise 1

Aim: to loosen the hips, lower back and spine.

Remove your pillow and lie flat on your back on the bed, with your legs straight and your hands palms-down and close to your side. Your fingers should be together and your toes pointing up.

Starting from the hip, slide your left leg slowly down past your right leg then slide it back.

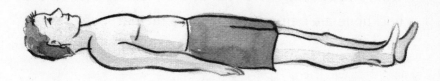

It is important to get this movement right, because it is the basis of many of the exercises that follow. What you are doing is pushing the leg downwards from the hip so that it extends for a few centimetres beyond the other leg. The movement at the hip is the key to it.

If you lie down on the floor and try it, you will understand at once what is involved. As you slide the leg down, you will feel your lower backbone engaged. What's happening here is that the muscles around the backbone are being stretched and the backbone flexed.

Repeat with the right leg.

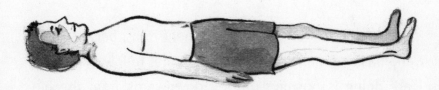

Exercise 2

Aim: to reset the spine and stretch the body gently.

As well as sliding your left leg slowly down past the other, roll it inwards from the hip as if you were trying to touch the mattress with the inside of your foot.

This is hard to do at first and you may take a few weeks to master it. Don't force the foot down. Just roll from the hip.

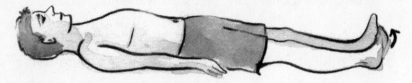

Repeat with the right leg.

Exercise 3

Aim: to stretch the lower back.

Lie flat on the bed and place both middle fingers on the pubic bone. (The fingers are put there purely as markers so you can see the pubic bone moving. They are not meant to play any part in the movement.)

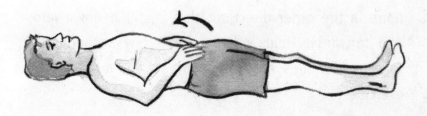

Thrust the pubic bone upwards—that is, as if you were trying to lift it towards your navel—without lifting your buttocks off the bed.

(Alternatively you can place your hands flat on the bed under the small of your back and flatten your back onto your hands.)   Hold it there for a few seconds and release. Repeat.

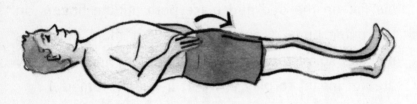

With your middle fingers still in place, move the pubic bone in the other direction; that is, tilt it downwards and forwards. Hold it there for a few seconds and release. The hips are not meant to be raised in this exercise.

Exercise 4

Aim: To release stiffness after lying in bed overnight.

Bend your left leg and place your left foot on the bed.

Now grasp the knee with both hands and gently draw it towards your chest, giving your lower spine a gradual stretch.

Hold the knee as close to the chest as possible for about fifteen seconds. Then let go and slowly return your foot to the bed.

Now repeat with the right leg.

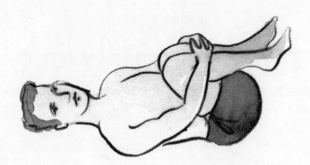

Grasp both knees with your hands, and bring them towards your chest, feeling a greater stretch in the lower back.

Hold the stretch for twenty to thirty seconds. Aim to eventually touch your knees to the chest without forcing the movement. You will notice improved flexibility as you repeat this exercise daily.

Now release your grip and return your feet to the bed slowly.

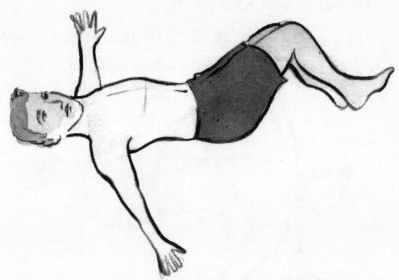

Place your arms out to ninety degrees from your body, so they rest on the mattress, and now keeping both knees together, roll the legs over to the left, aiming to touch the side of the left leg onto the mattress.

Try and keep the right arm flat on the bed and feel the stretch across your right chest and shoulder, and in the right side of your waist and hip.

Hold the stretch for fifteen seconds and then slowly return to the starting position.

Now repeat the movement towards the right side, and feel the stretch in the left side of your trunk. After fifteen seconds return to the starting position.

Exercise 5

Aim: to stretch the lower legs.

Bend both knees and place your feet flat on the bed, with your hands palm-down by your side and the fingers together.

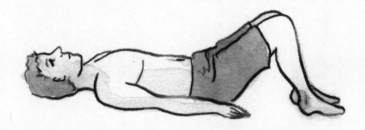

Squeeze toes down into mattress, then relax.

Flex the toes upward, then relax.

Exercise 6

Aim: To increase circulation and use the diaphragm
muscles correctly for breathing.

Bend both knees and place your hands on the front of
your abdomen with the fingers pointing down towards
the pubic area.

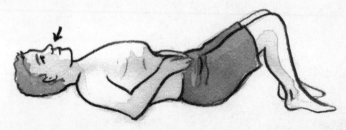

Breathe in slowly through your nose, allowing your torso to expand.

Breathe out slowly, allowing the torso to collapse. Repeat three times.

Exercise 7

Aim: to exercise the eyes.

Lie flat on the bed with the legs straight and flat and your eyes closed. Blink both eyes five times and then squeeze them shut firmly, keeping them squeezed for a few seconds. Release and repeat five times.

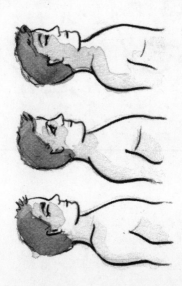

With the eyes still closed, look in turn upwards, to the right, downwards and to the left. Repeat in one direction (say, clockwise) and in the other (anti-clockwise).

Repeat Steps 1 and 2 with eyes open.

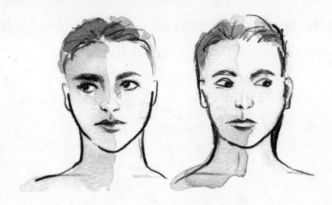

Exercise 8

Aim: to pelvic floor muscles.

Lying on your back with your knees bent, squeeze and lift and hold the pelvic floor muscles for as long as you can, then relax. Do not hold your breath and concentrate on squeezing and lifting up as you tighten the muscles. You will feel a light tension in your lower stomach muscles. Be careful not to tighten your upper stomach, buttocks or thighs (see page 35).

Rest for five seconds and repeat the exercise. Continue until the muscles feel tired. You're aiming to eventually be able to hold the contraction for about ten seconds and to do ten repetitions without tiring. Intensity is important, fewer good exercises will be more beneficial than several half-hearted ones.

Pelvic floor exercises can be done lying, sitting or standing.

Exercise 9

Aim: to exercise the neck.

Lying flat on the bed with your hands by your side and your toes pointing up, turn your head slowly to the right as far as comfortable before returning slowly to the starting point.

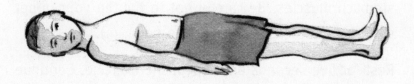

Slowly turn your head to the left as far as comfortable, then return to the starting point.

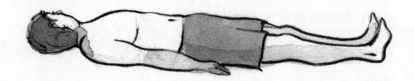

Exercise 10

Aim: To stretch the neck and reset the top
half of the spine.

Lie flat on the bed with your hands by your side and
your toes pointing up.

Raise your head slowly, then lower it slowly. Repeat five
times.

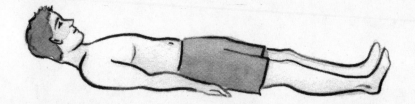

You are now ready to get out of bed and face the day! These exercises should take no time to complete and even on their own, can make quite a difference to your flexibility.

Standing Exercises

These can be done in the shower; if there isn't the space
in your shower, do the exercises straight after getting out
of the shower while you're still warm.

Exercise 1

Aim: to strengthen postural muscles.

While standing still, try and elongate your spine (i.e. grow tall) as if you have a piece of string pulling the top of your head towards the ceiling. Keep your shoulders relaxed, avoiding any temptation to elevate them. You should feel your chin glide slightly towards your neck as you 'grow tall'.

This helps to prevent the onset of a stooped posture and poked forward chin. The more you practice this the easier it will become. You will look and feel younger!

Exercise 2

Aim: to loosen the hip, pelvic and lower-back areas,
to strengthen the abdominal area and to stretch
the hamstrings.

Standing under a hot
shower (the heat helps the
muscle to stretch), bend
forwards from your waist
with your legs straight,
your arms crossed and
your hands on opposite
shoulders. Position
yourself so that the water
is running over your
lower back.

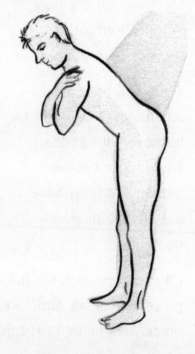

Keeping both legs straight—that is, the movement has to be initiated at the hip—lift each heel off the floor in turn. Hold for 15 seconds and repeat.

While still bent over, breathe in slowly and try to move your abdomen around in a circular motion. (At least have the mental image of doing it.)

Do it clockwise for a full circle and hold. Reverse the procedure in an anticlockwise direction. Repeat three times. This helps to readjust the organs in this area.

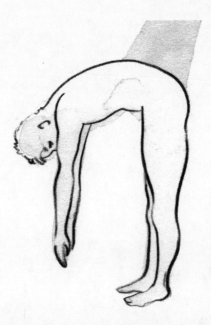

Then allow your shoulders and torso to relax and drop forward, stretching your lower back and hamstrings for a slow count of seven.

Afternoon or Evening Program

End the day with some stretches.

Exercise 1

Aim: to stretch the backbone after a day's sitting and to loosen the hips.

Lie flat on the floor with your toes pointing up, your arms and fingers outstretched above your head, as if you were trying to achieve your full height.

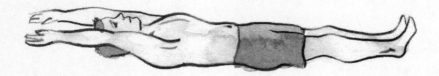

Sliding your left leg from the hip, slowly rotate it inwards and down, extending it past the right leg.

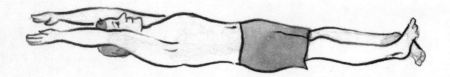

Return to starting position.

Sliding your right leg from the hip, slowly rotate it inwards and down, extending it past the left leg. Return to starting position.

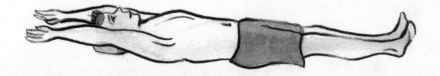

Exercise 2

Aim: to stretch the body, exercise the arm muscles and, by clenching and unclenching the fist, to pump blood through the arms.

Lie flat on the floor with your toes pointing up and your hands clenched by your sides.

While slowly extend each leg in turn from the hips, raise your arms over your head to full height, clenching and unclenching your fists as the arms swing over, as if you were squeezing a squash ball.

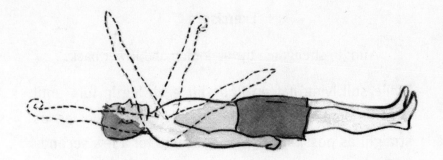

Return your arms to your sides slowly, clenching and unclenching your fists and extending alternate legs. The fist may be clenched and unclenched ten times each time the arm swings over. Breathe in each time you extend a leg, allowing the torso to expand. Raise your arms overhead and return them three times.

Exercise 3

Aim: to strengthen the abdomen and lower back.

While still lying flat on floor, lift each leg in turn until it is at right angles to the floor, keeping the leg as straight as possible, and hold it there for a few seconds before returning it to the floor.

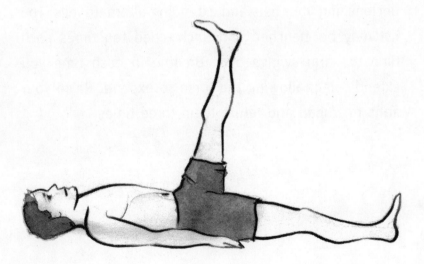

Lift both legs together to form a right angle with the bed, keeping the knees as straight as possible. Hold for a few seconds, then slowly lower.

Lift both legs together to form a right angle with the bed, hold briefly, then extend each leg in turn slowly from the hip.

Exercise 4

Aim: to strengthen the buttocks, lower back
and abdominal area

Roll over onto your stomach and place your hands by
your side.

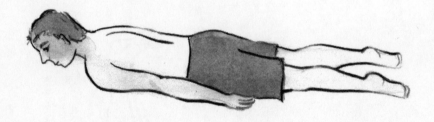

Raise your left leg, heel first, as far as is comfortable and hold for a few seconds. Return to the starting position.

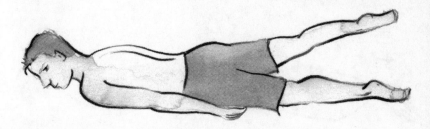

Repeat with the right leg.

With your hands by your sides, raise both legs together, heels first, and hold for a few seconds. Return.

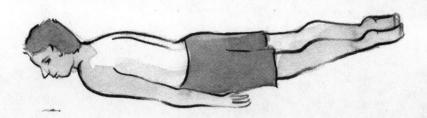

Stretch your arms over your head, cross the arms at the wrist and cross the legs at the ankles; then stretch your body for a slow count of five. Relax.

Exercise 5

Aim: to stretch and strengthen the stomach and
back muscles.

Roll over onto your back. Cross your arms, placing your
hands on opposite shoulders, and straighten your legs.

Raise your head and shoulders and hold for a few
seconds before relaxing. If it proves too difficult, however, bend your knees and then raise your head and
shoulders as far as comfortable, hold them there for a
few seconds before relaxing.

Exercise 6

Aim: to stretch and strengthen the stomach and lower
back muscles

Sit with your legs extended straight ahead. Lean forward
and extend the arms forward with outstretched fingers
and slowly work your torso towards your toes. Hold for
thirty seconds. Repeat.

Exercise 7

Aim: to stretch and strengthen the stomach and lower back muscles

Still sitting, place your hands behind you, fingers extended forwards and lower your body backwards as far as comfortable.

Exercise 8

Aim: to stretch and strengthen the stomach and lower
back muscles

Kneeling, sit upright on your heels with your hands in prayer position above your head. Keeping your elbows out, try to touch your shoulder blades together for a slow count of thirty seconds.

Exercise 9

Aim: to strengthen back and buttock muscles.

Lie on your back and bend your knees so that your feet are on the ground.

Lift your hips off the ground and hold your body in a straight line without sagging for fifteen seconds.

Slowly return to the floor and relax.

Repeat one more time. Your back and buttock muscles work to control your hips in this exercise.

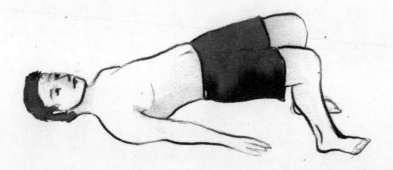

Muscle building

A man in his twenties or thirties can live like a slob and still look reasonably good, because his muscles and skeletal structure are young enough to maintain a respectable body shape. Beyond the age of fifty though, the way you live begins to show up in the way you look. If you fail to exercise your muscles they will start to visibly waste away. This is why even active middle-aged men can look scrawny or flabby from the waist up. They do enough walking to keep their legs well-muscled, but their upper body gets almost no exercise. This results in the familiar droop you see in middle-aged men: the chest sinks; the shoulders narrow and sag; the arms lose their muscular contours.

Upper body

To prevent this happening, you must take up some regular activity that gives the upper body a vigorous workout; you need to do weights or some equivalent exercise. As we all know, doing weights does involve a risk of injury— especially for someone over the age of fifty. By all means do weights in a gym under supervision, but if you do them at home make sure that what you're doing is safe.

Use your body weight

My own preference is not to do weights at all. Instead, I do chin-ups and pull-ups on a bar at home. There could hardly be simpler exercises than these, yet they're extremely effective in toning virtually every muscle in my upper body. I got the idea from Nigel Websdale — a fitness expert who has worked with sports people such as Pat Cash —

whom I got to know some years ago. I asked him to suggest a set of simple exercises that I could do regularly to keep my upper body in shape. I made it clear to him that I had no ambition to achieve athlete-type fitness. I just wanted to keep myself in reasonable health and in reasonable shape for the rest of my life.

Even so, I expected to be told to go out and buy a bench and weights or some other state-of-the-art body-building gear. Nigel said forget it— the only equipment I needed to obtain was a piece of galvanised iron pipe. I then had to find some place in or around my home where I could fasten it securely enough to bear my weight.

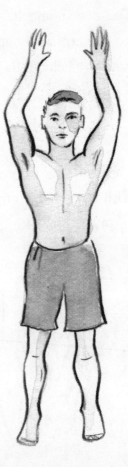

The bar should be securely positioned well above head height, preferably about level with the fingertips when the arms are held aloft.

Chin-ups and pull-ups

The chin-ups I do are of the traditional type. I do them with underhand grip on the bar; that is, with the palms of my hands facing me.

The pull-ups are virtually the same exercise, except that I have the palms facing the other way.

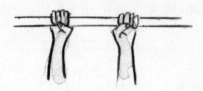

Between them, these two exercises ensure that all the muscles in the arms, chest and shoulders get a work-out.

Make sure you breathe out when you pull yourself up, then breathe in as you lower yourself.

Leg lifts

Here is a third exercise I do on the bar every second morning which is a variation of the others. It is for

those of you who are confidently completing the chin-ups and pull-ups.

Hang from the bar with outstretched arms and repeatedly raise your knees to waist height. This simple exercise tones up the abdominal muscles as well as the lower back, thighs and buttocks.

Raise your knees in three directions in turn. One, straight up so they are pointing directly ahead; two, at an angle to the left (towards mid-wicket, as a cricketer would say); three, at an angle to the right (towards extra cover).

The reason for doing this is that it means all the muscles, right across the abdomen, get exercised. This exercise is particularly valuable if you are trying to get rid of a pot belly and it is a good alternative to sit-ups and other abdominal exercises.

Do not pull your knees up rapidly. You will derive the most benefit from this exercise if you raise and lower them slowly.

Also, as with the chin-ups and pull-ups, breathe out when you do the hard bit (raising your knees) and breathe in when you lower them. The reason you do this is to prevent pressure building up inside the body. If you breathe in or just hold your breath when you exert yourself, your blood pressure will rise and you will also build up pressure in the lungs and abdomen. Breathing out releases the pressure.

How often?

I do one of these three exercises each day in a three-day cycle, which means I spend no more than five minutes on them per day, including the short breaks between the various sets. I do chin-ups one day, pull-ups next day, knee-raises the day after that.

Rotation

There is a good reason for doing them in rotation like this. Physiologists tell us that the process of toning our muscles occurs in two stages. In the first stage, the muscle is broken down by overwork during the exercise itself. In the second, the muscle recovers and grows after the exercise. In other words, the improvement is actually achieved after the exercise is over. So if you exercise the same set of muscles every day, you will not derive as much benefit as you will from a three- or four-day rotation. The muscles of even top endurance athletes go through a recovery phase after competing. For people taking part in an Iron Man event, for instance, the recovery phase can be as long as two weeks.

Don't panic if you can't do it

If you have not done any heavy lifting for some time, you may well struggle to do more than one or two chin-ups or pull-ups to start with. It doesn't matter how few you can manage at first. Make sure you do not do them all at once but, rather, break them up.

Gradual increase within your own limitations

Gradually build up over time within your own limitations. Having done the exercise for years, I can comfortably manage a total of ten chin-ups or pull-ups, spread over four to five sets. I could do more than this with a greater effort, but I feel this is quite sufficient for the purpose. Your own comfortable limit is unlikely to be the same as mine, but it doesn't really matter, provided the muscles get the exercise.

Slow and steady increases

I do the knee-raises in the same way. Remember to vary the direction in which you raise your knees. If you have not done the exercise before, you may well find that one or two will pull you up at first. Keep at it, and you ought to be able to increase the number bit by bit.

Better than weights

Chin-ups and pull-ups have one important advantage over weights: they are less likely to result in injuries to muscles and ligaments, for the simple reason that you never have to lift more than your body weight. If the strain becomes too great, you simply won't be able to pull yourself up. In other words, if you can't do it, you won't do it. Another big advantage is the simplicity of it all. With a piece of iron pipe a metre long you can create your own home gym. If you are even half a handyman you should have no trouble installing one somewhere inside or outside your home, and the materials you need — the length of pipe plus maybe a few screws and brackets — is next to nothing.

Keep on going

I am never particularly conscious of the benefits of these exercises while I'm doing them, but when I don't do them for a week or more because I'm away on a trip, I soon notice the difference. I can feel the loss of strength, muscle tone and bulk in and around my shoulders. Whenever I lose weight I tend to lose it first around the shoulders, so the exercises on the bar are all the more important for me.

Not long ago I spent the best part of a month travelling. I worked for twelve days in India on a cricket broadcast, came home for a day, went to Fiji for three days, came home for two days, then spent five days in New Zealand.

During the whole of that period I did no exercises at all on the bar. By the end of it I felt almost frail. It seemed to me that a strong wind would have blown me away. Yet after just one week back on the exercise bar I felt like Arnold Schwarzenegger. I didn't look like him, but I felt like him!

Muscle preservation

Feeling good as a result of exercising is actually very important. It is the carrot your body dangles in front of you: it gives you the incentive to keep going. So you exercise more because it makes you feel good, and all the while your body is reaping the benefit.

I personally believe that chin-ups and pull-ups are ideal for the particular needs of middle-aged men, especially the majority of us who shy away from the idea of going to a gym. Most of us past the age of fifty, quite sensibly, have given up the idea of trying to build up our bodies for the sake of appearance, and while these exercises on the bar may be muscle-building they are certainly not meant to be a form of body-building. The primary objective is not to develop bigger muscles today but to preserve the muscles you already have for the future.

You'll be amazed at how quickly you notice a difference. You'll feel the muscles in your shoulders and arms developing and you will feel stronger because of it. (You'll see the extra muscle in the mirror, too, which may appeal to your vanity.)

I do the muscle-toning exercises with the long-term objective in my mind that twenty or even thirty years from now I aim to have enough strength in my upper body to do all the things I still want to do, one of which, I'm sure, will be to make the golf ball fly off the tee instead of just bunting it along the fairway.

Making time

By and large, we are all too busy being busy. We live our lives at what seems to us a hectic pace, which we then use as an excuse for failing to do a lot of things we ought to do. If we were to sit down and put on paper everything we have left undone recently, most of us could fill a page. Our list would include all sorts of everyday items, each of them important in its own way yet none so urgent that it had to be done there and then, so it wasn't done.

Fitness always seems to be something we can worry about tomorrow.

Making an effort each day to keep fit may not be on everyone's list of things they should have done, but it ought to be, for the majority of Australian men neglect to do it.

Somehow, fitness always seems to be something we can worry about tomorrow.

The most important activity

The truth is, if we examine our daily schedules honestly, there's plenty of time each day to do all the things we've been putting off. The trouble is we fail to organise our time. The secret of finding time to do something is to make time to do it, not just vaguely hope that time might become available. You have to *deliberately* set aside time for it.

Our health is so important that we have to find the time for it in our schedules.

Admittedly there is a limit to how far we can go in putting all our waking hours into various boxes, but our physical fitness—and, therefore, our health—is so important, so vital to our overall wellbeing, that we have to make a box for it. It must be written into the daily schedule.

After retiring from cricket I concentrated on my second-favourite game, golf. I played every Saturday, yet, for me, this was not enough. It wasn't enough for me to improve my play, and it wasn't enough to satisfy my appetite for the game. I used to think how wonderful it would be to take Wednesday afternoons off, as many of my golfing friends did, and play in the usual mid-week competition.

If you don't plan you'll never have enough time and you won't ever get around to exercising.

But I was too busy, so I thought, and could not possibly afford the time.

One day I happened to mention to a fellow club member how I envied him being able to play on Wednesday. He replied, 'Mate, if you don't plan it, if you don't organise it, you'll never play on Wednesday, because you'll never have enough time.'

What he said set me thinking. I went back to the office and had my assistant draw a line through every Wednesday afternoon in my diary for weeks ahead. From then on I played in the Wednesday afternoon comp. It was not really a case of taking time off work to do it. I

Making time for exercise wasn't a case of taking time off work because I was already working 60 hour weeks.

was already working a sixty-hour week and continued to do so. Rather, it was a case of *making* time for it.

For a week or two, it did cause some disruption—a few appointments had to be changed and so on. After that my absence made no difference to how the office operated.

After all, if you leave the office to attend a meeting or some other appointment that lasts all afternoon, the office will continue to function. In other words, my Wednesday afternoon's golf was treated as just another appointment.

A productive break

What I also found interesting was the effect the afternoon's golf had on me. I'm sure I achieved a lot more by having that break in the middle of the week, because I always felt rejuvenated after it. The Wednesday golf was six hours away from the stress of life, and each week I found myself looking forward to it.

I made an appointment for myself to enjoy an activity which was exercise.

The point of all this is that I made time to do it. I made an appointment for myself to enjoy an activity which was exercise. This is what you might think of doing, too. If the only time you can walk or exercise is in the morning before you go to work, then get up half an hour earlier to do it. If your reply to this is, 'But I already have to get up at 6.00 a.m. to make it to work on time,' then my reply would be, 'So get up at 5.30!' Your fitness and your health are far, far too important to be treated as an expendable filler which you squeeze in somewhere when you have spare time. Make an appointment for yourself, in writing if necessary, to work on your fitness.

The cost of hard work

There is a crazy logic in the way many men lead their lives. They're so busy that they have no time to exercise. Their consciences are clear, because they feel they're doing the right thing by their families: making more money and providing their families with extra material benefits. Their consciences should not be clear, however.

By ignoring their health, most men are running a significant risk of being stricken by ill health and perhaps even dying in their fifties or sixties. The dire consequences both for their family and their work, if either possibility were to eventuate, are well known to us all. Viewed in this way, the man who can't find the time to devote to his health is grossly irresponsible. So you owe it to yourself to start exercising, today!